WHY KNOT US

A Story of Loss, Faith and the Unbreakable Knot that Held it Together

SHAWN PATRICK

Why Knot Us

Copyright © 2025 by Shawn Patrick

Paperback ISBN: 978-1-963732-20-7

Hardback: 978-1-963732-21-4

Published by

The Publishing Pad

www.thepublishingpad.com

Table of Contents

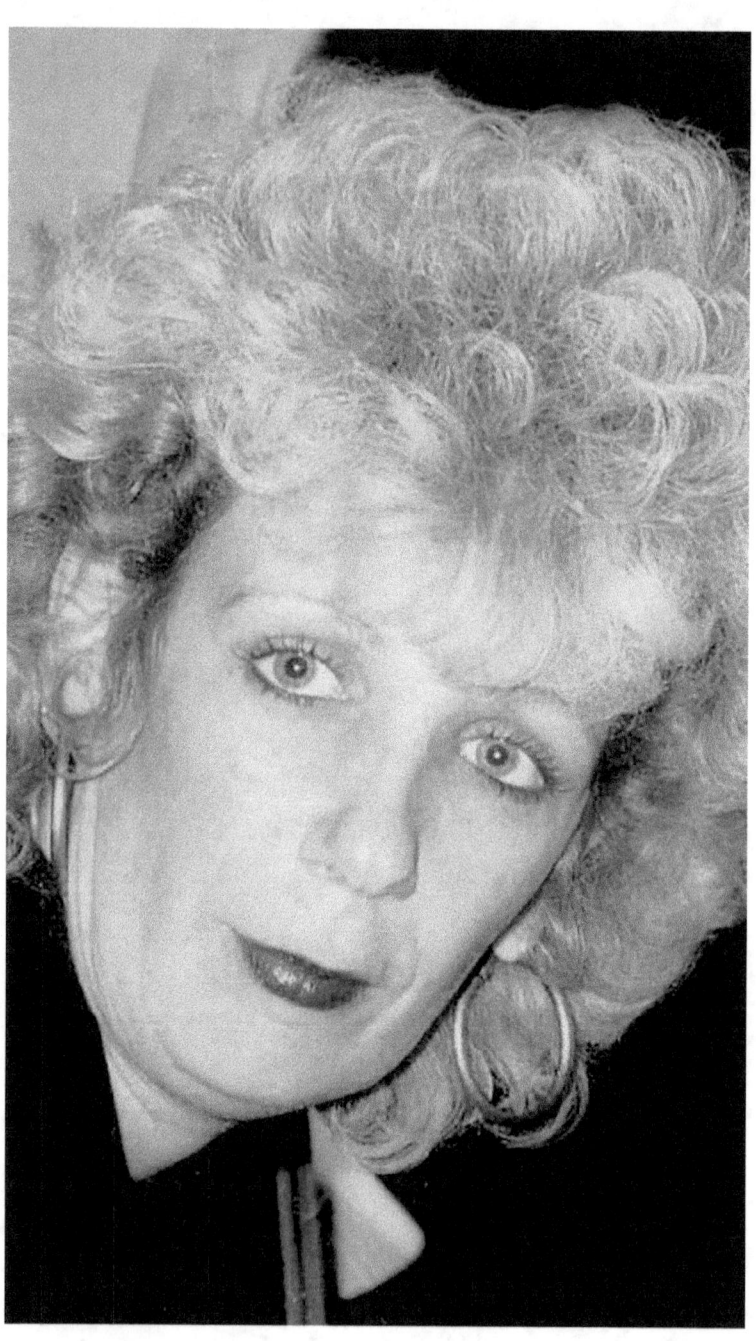

CHAPTER 1

The End of The Beginning

It was October 21st, 2001, the day everything changed. I was thirteen years old, just a kid living in a small town called Albertson in New York, right on the border between Queens and Long Island. My world back then was small: my older brother Rob, my father Bobby, and my mother Barbara.

Mom was the heart of our home. I always knew she was sick, but I didn't know how sick. At that age, you think pain is something that goes away with sleep or soup. You don't understand terminal illness. You don't understand the kind of pain someone hides with a smile. Mom hid it well, too well.

Dad was drinking a lot around that time. He'd come home late, eyes red, heart heavy. I know now it wasn't just the alcohol. It was the weight of watching the woman he loved fade away, day by day. But I didn't get it back then. I just thought he was angry, tired, maybe even mad at us. But really, he was just breaking in silence.

A nurse named Pauline started coming by the house for a few weeks. She wore a name tag with the word "Hospice" on it. I thought that was just the name of her company. I didn't know it meant the end was near. Nobody explained that to a 13-year-old.

That afternoon, the house was full. My Aunt Nancy, my grandmother, my uncles—all of my mom's side were there, even the nurse. I remember thinking it was strange for everyone to be over at once, but I figured it was just one of those "family visits."

Dad was in the backyard, pacing, lost in himself. He didn't look right, like something was wrong under his skin. I thought maybe he was just having another bad day, probably had a drink or two. I didn't realize he already knew what I was about to find out.

Inside, Mom was sitting on her usual spot on the couch, wrapped in her brown wool blanket—the one she always used because she got cold so easily. I used to tuck it around her whenever she was shivering. That blanket smelled like her. It felt like her.

She looked at me and said something she'd told me many times before, but this time it stuck deeper: "Shawn, anytime you find a dime on the floor, that means an angel is watching over you. Don't spend them... save them. More dimes, more angels."

I didn't know it yet, but those would be the last words she ever said to me.

Later that day, I was in my room, sitting at the computer— just a normal moment in a not-so-normal house—when I suddenly heard it. My grandmother screaming. My family crying.

I ran into the living room, heart pounding. There were people crowding the couch, blocking her from view. I pushed through. I saw Mom slumped over, still wrapped in the brown blanket, but her head was down. Silent.

My aunt turned to me and said words I didn't fully understand at the time. "Shawn, your mom has passed away."

Passed away. I'd only seen people die in movies. I stood there frozen. Then I ran.

I ran out of the house, down the block, into a nearby park. I saw one of my friends named Sean who was there with his father, shooting hoops. I could barely speak, but I told them, "My Aunt said my mom died."

It didn't feel real. None of it did. Just thirteen years old, and the light of my life had gone out.

I slept in my mother's bed that night. The smell of her blanket, the empty side of the bed — it haunted me. I didn't sleep. I just existed.

I never saw her open her eyes again. But I started finding dimes.

CHAPTER 2

Dimes

The next morning after Mom passed, the world didn't stop but it felt like it should've.

My brother Rob, who was four years older than me, had a girlfriend at the time, and that's where he went to cope. I didn't blame him. He was driving already, old enough to leave. I guess everyone was just trying to survive in their own way.

Dad? He was in pieces.

My Aunt Linda, Dad's sister, showed up with a box of Dunkin' Donuts. I'll never forget the confusion on her face when she asked me, "Where's your dad?" A few hours later, we found out he had gotten arrested for driving drunk the night before. Mom was gone. Rob was with his girlfriend. And now Dad was locked up. I remember thinking, "This isn't real. This feels like a movie." But it wasn't.

Time passed. The drinking didn't stop. In fact, it got worse. Dad became more bitter, more lost, angry at the world and probably angry at himself.

But Aunt Linda kept showing up. Quietly, consistently. Checking in. She was a light in the middle of a storm—I'll speak more about her later, because she deserves her own chapter.

Meanwhile, the roles started to flip. I was the one waiting up at night, listening for the door, hoping Dad made it home safe. And when he did, I was the one tucking him in, waiting for his breath to slow and his eyes to close.

I was thirteen.

I was the kid.

But I became the adult.

When high school started, it didn't feel like a fresh chapter, it felt like a spotlight. Everyone looked at me like "That's the kid who lost his mom." And I didn't want to be that kid. So I disappeared.

I stopped going to school. I'd leave the house and just head to the park, shooting hoops all day. That orange basketball was the only thing that felt simple. It didn't ask questions. It didn't stare. It just bounced and came back to me.

A few months into this new reality, Dad's side of the family—my grandma (we called her Mema) and Aunt Pat—reached out. They lived in Naples, Florida, and they wanted us to move down there to be closer and to start over.

It sounded good on paper: palm trees, a slower pace, family support. But I still felt alone. Then something changed.

We got a dog.

He was half Dalmatian, half Pointer—face split right down the middle: one side black, one side white. Even his butt was

half black, half white. He looked like he was painted by angels with shaky hands.

We needed another heartbeat in the house, something living to keep us from going numb.

When we met him, I knew.

Dad asked, "Who is he?"

And I said, "That's Dimes." He was staring at me with this goofy look, tongue hanging out, like he already loved me.

From that day on, Dimes became my best friend.

Rob still had his girlfriend.

Dad still had his bottle of wine.

And I had Dimes.

He was loyal from day one. Even when he'd pee on the floor because he wasn't trained yet, and Dad, drunk and angry, would throw him out the front door yelling, "That'll teach him!" Dimes still came back.

He'd bark. Scratch. Wag his tail. Lick Dad's hand.

He never held a grudge. He just kept loving. Looking back, it's like he knew we were all broken. But he stayed. Loyal. Brave. Forgiving.

Just like Mom said, "More dimes, more angels." I had one. And he had four legs.

CHAPTER 3

Fresh Start, or Not

We packed up everything we had into one moving truck. We were moving to Florida to stay close to grandma and Aunt Pat. No backseat. Just Dad, Rob, me, and Dimes—our black-and-white angel with the long tongue and zero manners. Dimes was drooling on everyone.

Dad was driving. Rob sat passenger. I squeezed in the middle with a pile of fur and love laying across my lap. My brother was already annoyed. Dad was getting mad by the mile.

Finally, after one too many splats of warm slobber, Dad screamed, "Dimes! Keep your damn mouth shut!"

Dimes looked at him with the most confused, sideways head tilt—tongue hanging long like a wet sock—and without missing a beat, let loose a massive string of drool right into Dad's eye. Dad pulled over, completely blind. Couldn't see a thing. Eyes full of dog spit.

Rob and I looked at each other—both trying to stay serious—but I felt it coming. That laugh. That first real laugh

since Mom died. I reached for the door lock, just in case Dad tried to throw Dimes out. But we all just sat there...

And we laughed.

Hard. Together.

Like we used to.

·•●•·

Florida didn't feel like home.

We got a place near Mema's house, but it was nothing like New York. You couldn't walk anywhere. Everything was spread out. Wide roads. Palm trees. Empty sidewalks. It felt like a dream you weren't supposed to be in.

Rob missed his girlfriend the minute we got there. Dad kept drinking, maybe even more than before. And the fights started. Rob and I were always at each other's throats. Not because we hated each other, but because we were both hurting, and Mom wasn't there to break it up. She was the glue. Without her, everything started to split.

Then came my first day of school. I didn't know a soul. No one talked like me. No one dressed like me. After first period, I heard something I thought was a joke. "Okay, it's cookie break time!"

I turned to the kid sitting next to me. He looked like he just stepped off a surfboard—tan, long hair, sandals, toes out. I was wearing a Knicks jersey and Jordans, fresh from the city.

"Did that lady just say cookie break time?" I asked. He looked at me, squinted, and went, "Yeah, brah. Cookie break time."

What?!

Where I came from, break time meant cutting class and finding a basketball court. Here? They had cookie stations on every corner. You couldn't even ditch class if you tried—cookies were blocking all exits.

I felt like I had landed on a different planet.

•• ● ••

Home wasn't much better.

Dad kept drinking. Rob kept brooding. I kept trying to find somewhere I belonged, and I wasn't finding it at school or home. But there was one thing that made every day worth it:

Dimes.

That dog met me at the door every day like I was a hero. Didn't matter how bad school was. Didn't matter how bad Dad smelled like wine or how many fights I had with Rob. Dimes was there. Tongue out. Tail wagging. Loyal.

We went to Mema's house often. She lived with Aunt Pat, and they'd cook us dinner. Fried this, baked that—real comfort food. They tried to make it feel like home. And it helped. But it still wasn't home. No subway. No courts. No corners. No Ma.

Just palm trees. Sandals. And a cookie break.

CHAPTER 4

No Long Goodbyes

R ob still couldn't find his way. He was 18, stuck between becoming a man and holding onto the pieces of a life that used to make sense. And palm trees weren't helping him either.

He didn't have his girlfriend anymore. Dad still had his bottle. And I had Dimes.

A couple weeks into Florida, Rob picked me up in his car. It was one of his favorite things—his cars. That was his passion. He'd buy them cheap, clean them up, fix whatever was broken, and flip them for cash. He was like a mechanic with a hustle. Always moving metal. They say your first word says a lot about you. Rob's first word was "Mitsubishi."

We hit McDonald's that afternoon. I had a Big Mac and a large Coke, the kind where the ice hits the back of your teeth. I remember it so clearly, because what happened next carved into me like a scar.

As we pulled back into the driveway, I looked up at the house and saw Dimes in the window, watching, waiting. I was

just about to open the car door when Rob said, "Stay in the
car. We need to talk."

I figured maybe we were making birthday plans—I was
about to turn 14. But it wasn't that.

He said, "I can't do this anymore, Shawn. I'm going back
to New York. I'm gonna stay with Aunt Nancy... and be with
my girlfriend. I just... I can't be here."

I sat frozen. The Coke still in my hand. We had fought like
brothers do—loud, stupid, and often. But through it all, we
were still together. Still family. Now he was telling me he was
leaving. It felt like losing someone all over again.

Before I could stop myself, I took the lid off my drink and
poured the entire large Coke all over his driver seat.

It wasn't about the soda. It was about everything.

He looked at me, and I'll never forget that look. It wasn't
anger. It was something worse. It was final.

I stormed into my room and shut the door. Dimes followed,
like always. He lay next to me, quiet. Even he could feel
something was different.

After a while, when the house felt still again, I walked down
the hall. I knocked on Rob's door.

Nothing. Knocked again. Dimes barked. Still nothing.
I thought he was just ignoring me. So I slowly pushed the
door open...

Drawers empty. Pillows gone.

I ran to the window. His car was gone. I ran to the kitchen,
and there it was. A note on the table. No long goodbye. No
explanation. Just what it was.

"Went back to New York."

I tried calling.

No answer.

No text.

No word.

I knew I had pushed too far. I knew I poured more than soda that day—I poured out everything I'd been holding in.

And just like that, another piece of my family was gone.

CHAPTER 5

Mema's House

After Rob left, things got heavy—too heavy—in that Florida apartment. It was just me, Dad, and Dimes. So we packed what little we had and moved into Mema's house.

Mema lived with Aunt Pat and Wayne, my little cousin—he was maybe eight at the time. They had a little Jack Russell Terrier named Gretta—all attitude, no size. Now we were one big, mismatched crew under one roof: Mema, Aunt Pat, Wayne, my dad, me, Dimes, and Gretta.

Dad and I slept on the pullout couch in the living room—every night, our home folded into the middle of the house. The tension? Always folded in with it.

I hated school. Dad couldn't find steady work. Everyone was stepping on each other's toes. It felt like one spark away from a fire.

And Mema didn't play. She was tough, classic New York tough. She ran that house like a sergeant in slippers. If you acted up? A shoe to the back of the head wasn't out of the question. But behind the sharp tongue and flying sandals, she was the

glue. Without her, that house would've fallen apart faster than we already were.

Then came Super Bowl Sunday.

Dad had been out most of the night. I stayed up, waiting for him—quietly, because you don't wake Mema up after 9 p.m. unless it's life or death. I remember lying on the pullout couch, Dimes curled up next to me, ears perked. I kept peeking out the window, waiting for the headlights to hit the driveway.

Eventually, I saw it—Dad's white Buick, beat-up but familiar.

I exhaled. He made it home. But something didn't look right. I stepped outside to check. What I saw made my stomach drop. The passenger mirror was gone, the antenna bent like a pretzel, dents all over the body. It looked like the car had been in a bar fight and lost.

I ran inside, shook my dad awake. "Dad... what happened to the car?" He blinked, disoriented. Looked at me. Looked past me.

I asked again. "Dad... what happened?"

He just stared—not confused like he was lying, but confused like he really didn't know. And I believed him.

We stayed there for a moment, in silence. Me standing. Him sitting. Two faces stuck in a moment neither of us could explain. But in that moment... something broke.

Not the kind of break that shatters —

The kind of break that opens a door.

It was the first time I saw in my dad's face what I had been feeling in mine for years. The "What is happening to our lives?" question.

That night — that Super Bowl Sunday —

The booze stopped.

The lies stopped.

The mirror was already gone, but my dad finally started seeing himself clearly.

I was in my senior year of high school by then. Still flunking most of my classes. No idea how I was going to graduate. No idea what was next.

But something shifted in Dad after that night.

The next morning, he walked into an AA meeting.

Then he went back the next day.

And the next.

And the next.

At first, I thought he was just trying to stay sober.

But then I realized that he kept going because he saw himself in others, and he wanted to help them rise the way he was trying to.

It became more than recovery. It became redemption.

Life didn't get perfect... but it started getting possible.

And while things were starting to look up for dad...

I was still stuck in Florida,

no friends, no diploma, no plan...

and no idea how the hell I was going to graduate.

Shawn
Patrick

CHAPTER 6

A poem from Pain

They said I wouldn't graduate unless I wrote a poem. My English teacher looked me in the eye and told me straight, "You need to turn in this poem. And if you don't get an A... you're not graduating."

I didn't roll my eyes or crack a joke that day. I went home, laced up my basketball shoes, and grabbed a piece of paper. Then I sat down and started writing. But it didn't feel like I was writing. It felt like something was already written inside me, waiting to come out.

I picked up the pen. I let it bleed. I didn't revise it. I didn't overthink it. I just read it once and knew. This was it.

The next day, I showed up thinking I was going to hand it in, let the teacher read it quietly at her desk, maybe say, "Shawn, good job."

But nope. She said, "Every student will now read their poem... in front of the entire graduating class." Over a hundred kids.

One by one, they went up to the mic. Some read about their vacations. Some read about roses and violets. Others talked about surfing and how high the water gets in Florida.

And then I heard it. "Next up... Shawn Patrick"

My heart dropped. But in my New York mind, I said, "F**k it... Let's get it." I stood up, walked to the mic, head high.

I already stood out by having a buzz cut because I shaved my hair when Mom lost hers to chemo—just so she wouldn't feel alone. I was used to standing out. But this? This was different.

I cleared my throat. And I began:

> *October 21 was a bad day.*
> *I thought I was losing my life—*
> *the same way my dad was losing his wife.*
> *I wanted to grab a knife and end the pain,*
> *drowning in fears,*
> *drenched in tears,*
> *like it was a race—*
> *to see what could hurt me faster.*
> *I'm no master of the perfect life.*
> *It's like when your dad comes home late*
> *because he misses his mate.*
> *It's like fishing without bait*
> *just trying to open a new gate,*
> *a new date,*
> *a new place to live.*
> *But it's hard...*
> *I'm so poor,*

I don't even have one hand to give.
Still, I've gotta forgive God
For the things He's done.
All I want
is to connect as four
and unite as one.
And I am so proud to say...
I am my mother's son.
Because in my heart,
she will always be
number one.

The room went dead silent. You could hear a pin drop.
I looked up...
Teachers were crying. Every single one of them.
But to be honest?
It didn't faze me.
I wasn't trying to impress anyone.
I was just telling them my life.
And here's the craziest part —
When the teacher came up to me and asked for a copy of
my poem...
I gave her the paper.
But there was something missing.
It was blank, except for my name at the top. I'd written a
short piece the night before, but I ripped it just before going
up to that mic. Every single word I said there, came straight
from my heart.

She looked at me, hugged me hard, and said, "Congratulations. I'll see you at graduation."

To this day, I don't know if it was pity, or if I wrote the poem of a lifetime.

Either way?

I'll take that diploma.

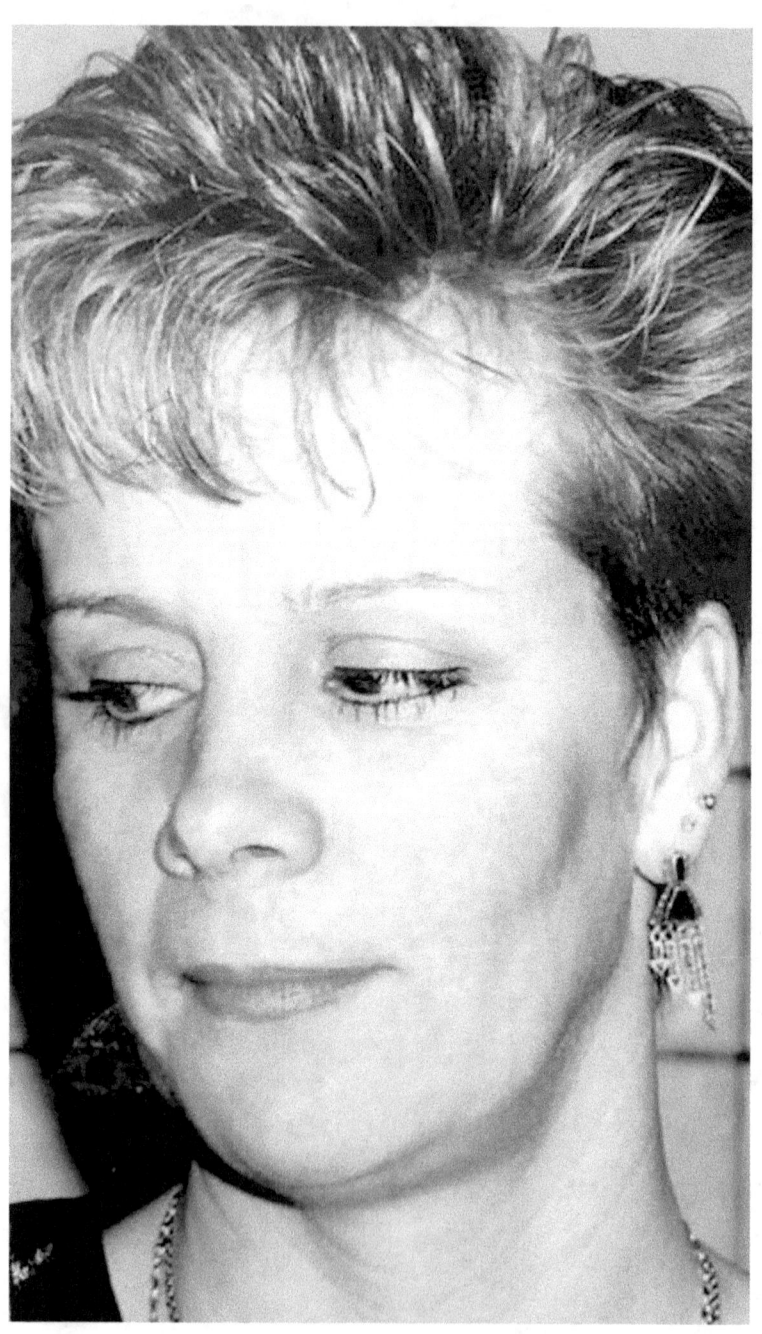

CHAPTER 7

Aunt Linda's house

After I graduated, things felt steady—for a while. Dad was sober, two years strong, hitting meetings every single day. Me and Dimes were still tight as ever—my boy, my shadow, my therapy. I started to adjust a bit to Florida. The weather didn't feel as foreign, and Mema and Aunt Pat were giving me structure.

Mema, she stepped up big. She was more than my grandma. She was my second mom, my compass, my balance. After graduation, I stayed with her. Still didn't know what the hell I was gonna do with my life, but I knew I needed to figure it out.

Then the phone rang. It was Aunt Pat. She said, "Shawn... Mema passed away." She smoked heavy. Always had. But like Mom, I didn't realize how bad it was. Or maybe I just didn't want to.

At the funeral, I kept running to the bathroom, throwing up, shaking. At one point, I dropped to my knees in that funeral bathroom, head over the toilet, tears falling onto the tile. And

I looked up at the ceiling like I was looking for God Himself, and I said, "Why?"

That was the moment I understood something real —
Nothing lasts forever.

That funeral broke me. It made me feel like I had nothing left to lose.

And that's a dangerous place to be.

Not long after that, I found out Rob was moving back to Naples with Aunt Nancy. He was over New York. But me? I was ready to go back. I had a white Jeep, a few dollars in my pocket, and a plan: Go back to NYC. Get a place. Get Dimes. Get my life together.

I left Dimes with Aunt Pat, promising I'd come back for him. I had to go alone this time. I was 17, and I needed to stand on my own two feet. Halfway up, somewhere in South Carolina, my phone rang. It was Rob. "Dad got locked up."

He told me a guy from Dad's AA meetings, someone Dad had been trying to help, got drunk and started disrespecting Mom's name. And you don't do that around a Brooklyn guy who's lost everything. Dad slapped him. Didn't punch. Just slapped. Still got arrested.

I had two choices: Turn around, or keep driving. I knew Dad would be okay. So I kept going.

I pulled up to Aunt Linda's—the same woman who brought me Dunkin' Donuts the day after Mom died.

She opened the door, and before I even said anything, she said, "You can stay on the couch as long as you need." No judgment. No questions. Just love.

· · ● · ·

Now I needed money. No job. No resume. Just hunger. That's when Kevin entered the picture.

Kevin was a legend. Certified hustler.

Bootleg shirts at football games.

Teddy bears and roses on Valentine's Day.

And for Mets games at Shea Stadium? He made mobile BBQ grills out of shopping carts and sold hot pretzels outside.

One day he said, "You tryna learn the game or what?"

Aunt Linda begged me, "Shawn, stay away from Kevin."

But I needed out. So I said yes.

And in my first hour, I made a few hundred dollars. And I knew right then: I'm never working a 9-to-5.

That year, the Giants won the Super Bowl.

Kevin went all in. Ordered over 500 shirts that said, "Giants Super Bowl Champs." Set up a table right outside the victory parade.

He handed me a stack and said, "Shawn, stand here and yell: Twenty dollars, get your shirts here!"

I did it. And the crowd surrounded me like bees on honey.

I was on fire. I had three thousand dollars in my pockets in under twenty minutes. I was dreaming about a new place to live. I was thinking about going back to get Dimes. I was thinking about finally building something real.

I looked over to find Kevin. He wasn't working. He was just leaning on a street pole in the corner, smoking a Newport, grinning at me like a proud coach.

Then it happened.

A woman came up to me, held up a shirt. "How much?"

I said, "For you? Twenty."

She smiled and said, "Great." Then she pulled out a badge. Next thing I know, I'm in handcuffs.

Undercover cops everywhere. Put me against the wall, reading me my rights like I was a threat.

I looked around the corner —

Kevin was still standing there, still smoking that cigarette, just watching.

Didn't flinch.

Didn't move.

Didn't say a word.

And in that moment, I realized the truth: In this life... all you got is yourself.

CHAPTER 8

Standing Alone

You'd think after getting arrested at the Giants' Super Bowl parade, I would've learned my lesson. I had money in my pocket. And after that kind of rush, after that kind of high, there's no punching a clock at some regular job.

I couldn't live like that. I wasn't built for it.

I started watching people more—how they moved, how they reacted. I was learning poker, but I had already been gambling on myself my whole life. Reading faces. Taking chances. Playing with fire.

I found a few underground games.

My new routine?

Treat myself to a nice dinner.

Wear something clean.

Pull up to the table with steel nerves and no fear.

Win money. Go home.

I felt invincible. I was still hustling—still selling at Giants Stadium and Shea, even after what Kevin did. But at the end of the day, Kevin taught me survival.

Not drugs. Not crime.

The street game. The hustle.

And that was something I could never repay him for.

Still, I had Aunt Linda whispering in my ear, "Shawn...
you better stop."

But I felt like she just didn't understand. Truth is — she
did. And she loved me enough to keep warning me.

Back then, I wasn't close with Dad or Rob. They were still
down in Florida, trying to figure life out. I was in New York,
trying to build mine—my way. I played ball every day. And
that's how I met Steve.

Cool kid, smooth talker.

One day he asked me what I did. I opened my trunk—hats,
shirts, pretzels stacked neatly inside—and said, "This is what I
do. Daytime hustle. Nighttime poker."

No drugs.

No drinking.

Just money moves.

· · ● · ·

One night, Steve asked me to hit a bar. He was driving.

We pulled up, and at the door, I saw Richard, a retired cop,
and father of one of my best friends—a man I respected like
family. I also slept on his couch time to time.

He looked at me, nodded, and asked, "Who you with?"

I said, "Steve. Kid from basketball."

Richard didn't hesitate. "He's trouble. Don't go home
with him."

I said, "Nah, he's good. I got him."

He gave me that look. That "I'm warning you, kid" kind of look.

I should've listened. But I didn't.

On the way home, we got pulled over. I was in the passenger seat, window halfway down, when two men in football jerseys came sprinting up to the car. They weren't in uniform. No badges.

They opened my door and tried to rip me out of the car. I fought back. Steve panicked and hit the gas. The guys lost grip and we sped off—but not far.

We turned the corner and hit a roadblock. Twenty-five police cars. Surrounding us. Lights flashing. Guns drawn. They yanked me out of the car. Punched me twice. Screamed, "Where's the drugs?!"

I kept shouting, "What drugs?! What drugs?!"

They found nothing. Because there was nothing. They locked me up anyway. Me in one cell. Steve in another.

All I could do was sit and think.

About Aunt Linda's warnings.

About Kevin.

About Richard at the door of that bar.

Three signs.

Three voices.

All ignored.

And now I was sitting in a cold cell, alone. Facing everything.

That night, something cracked open in me. I realized I'd been riding the fast horse way too long.

I had to move differently.
New people.
New choices.
New rules.
I wasn't close to my dad.
Wasn't close to Rob.
Wasn't even close to God.
Just me. Standing alone.
Trying to figure out if this life I was building...
Was even worth it.

CHAPTER 9

Why Knot Us

A few years went by.
Life quieted down—not easier, just... different.

I got into the hospitality business. Started as a server, and something about it came naturally. The smooth talking. The charm. The hustle. I was good at it.

But I didn't get there alone. It was Aunt Linda—the one who never gave up on me—who put me on game. She taught me everything about restaurants, from how to carry a tray to how to read a customer from top to bottom.

Even when I didn't listen, she still saved me.

Dimes was still down in Florida with Dad. They got closer over time—the bond between a man and a dog with too much history to explain.

I was making good money, finally getting some rhythm. Still crashing at Aunt Linda's house from time to time.

Then one day, I got a call. It was Nicole. Aunt Linda's daughter.

"Aunt Linda passed away. Cancer," she said

Just like that.

Another mother figure.

Another light in my life — gone.

Every person I get close to dies.

My body went numb.

I locked myself in the bathroom.

Dropped to my knees.

Looked up. "Why, God? Is this all a test?"

· · ● · ·

Back in Florida, Dad was still sober. Rob found a good woman, and they decided to move back to New York.

It felt like a full-circle moment. Only this time, Dimes was older — tongue still out, still loyal, but slowing down.

Rob got his own place. I moved back in with Dad in Florida. Then Covid hit. We were locked in the house. No distractions. No escape.

At first, it was quiet. Tense. Still some resentment from the past. But over time, we talked.

One night.

Then another.

Then something changed.

We realized there's no manual for losing a mother.

No rulebook for losing a wife.

Or a sister.

There's only family —

And the choice to forgive.

· · ● · ·

Rob got married.

Had a son.

Moved close to me and Dad.

And for the first time in a long time...

We were whole.

Then Dimes started to fade.

He couldn't walk.

His eyes looked tired.

We took him to the vet.

The doctor looked us in the eye and said, "It's everywhere. Cancer. It's time." We had to let him go.

That dog carried me through more pain than I ever want to relive. He was the only heartbeat that never left my side. He was named because of Mom. And he was my best friend.

That day, when we said goodbye, I watched my father cry for the first time in my life.

Dad and I lost our jobs because of Covid.

So we got in the car and drove.

Back to Naples.

No plan—just movement.

We ended up at the beach.

The sky was blue.

Yachts passed.

Kids laughed.

Behind us: mansions, champagne, and comfort.

My dad looked me dead in my eye and said, "I'm sorry we're not living like these people."

But me?

I didn't care.

I had him.

I had Rob.

And for once, I had peace.

So I looked back at him and said, "Why not us?"

He paused.

I said it again. "Why NOT us?"

And in that moment, a lightbulb.

A feeling I'd never felt before.

· · ● · ·

On the ride back to New York, we listened to an audiobook: "Three Feet From Gold."

I wasn't even focused on the story—I was holding a pen. I grabbed a scrap of paper and wrote one word: WHY. Then I drew a knot. A tight rope twist—one you can't pull apart. Below that, I wrote: US

And suddenly, it all hit me: WhyKnotUS

That knot was every ounce of pain I held onto.

That rope was family, tied back together.

That moment—that name—became everything I'd been searching for.

But life wasn't done with me yet.

We got back to New York, and Rob had a doctor's appointment. Just a check-up. Nothing serious. He was healthy. That's what we thought.

Then he told us, "I have melanoma." Skin cancer.

CHAPTER 10

The Promise

S ome time passed, and things felt... heavy again.
Rob sat us down one day. His face was calm, but his eyes
told a different story. "The cancer... it's in my lungs now."

But then he said something that gave us hope, "They're
going to do a procedure. It's highly effective. There's a good
chance I'll be okay."

He said it with strength. He said it with belief. So we held
onto that. What he didn't know was that Dad had just gotten
news, too.

A spot on his spleen.

They both kept quiet about it.

Didn't want to stress each other out.

But I was in the middle —

Knowing both truths.

Carrying both secrets.

With no one I could tell.

Rob was starting chemo in a week.

Dad had a procedure scheduled the week after.

Every day, I went to see Rob in the hospital in Manhattan.

Room after room. Elevator after elevator.

Same walk. Same routine.

But this wasn't just a visit. It was a mission.

When I got there, I'd help him out of bed —

Gown on. IV machine rolling beside us.

We'd walk a slow lap through the hospital corridors to get his legs moving again.

And at the end of that lap...

There were these chairs.

Nothing fancy—just two seats next to a wall of glass.

You sit down...

and you see the skyline of New York City laid out in front of you like a painting.

Steel. Light. Motion.

It looked so alive... while he was fighting to stay that way.

One day, we were sitting in those chairs.

Rob looked tired.

His face was pale, but focused.

He looked out at the city, then turned to me and said: "Shawn... if anything ever happens to me... I need you to finish WhyKnotUS. And I need you to be in my son's life. Give him the life we didn't have."

I froze.

Not because I was afraid. But because I understood what that moment meant.

His son... born on my birthday. July 18. And his name?
Robbie Dimes Tracy.

Robbie — after my brother.

Dimes — after my mother

Tracy — after the name we all fight to honor, our
family name.

I looked at Rob.

He had tubes in his arms, wires running to machines, the
city glowing behind him...

And I felt everything stop.

But I didn't flinch.

I couldn't.

I just nodded.

Held it together.

Because this wasn't just about a brand.

This was about blood.

This was about a promise.

A promise to carry the name.

To raise that boy right.

To finish what we started.

To take everything we lost, and turn it into something the
world could never ignore.

CHAPTER 11

Breaking Point

D ad was scheduled for surgery the day before Rob was
set to leave the hospital after finishing his final chemo
treatment.

It was supposed to be simple. Just a procedure to remove a
small spot on his spleen.

Before they wheeled him into the operating room, Dad
looked at me and said, "Once I'm in... go be with Rob."

But I couldn't be in two places at once. I had to choose.
So while Dad was under anesthesia, I sat in the hospital
hallway... waiting. Thinking it was routine. Thinking I'd be
with Rob soon.

Then my phone rang. It was the surgeon.

"Is this Shawn Patrick?"

I said yes.

"Just confirming. Your father — Robert?"

"Yes."

Then came the words that dropped my stomach to the
floor. "We planned to take a small piece out of his spleen...

But the cancer traveled everywhere. It's spread across his entire stomach. It's stuck to the walls. We have to take out a lot more than expected."

And then he paused.

His voice wasn't calm.

It was shaky. Rattled.

Like he didn't know how to process what he found inside my father.

And then...

He hung up.

I sat there frozen.

Phone still in my hand.

Mouth dry. Heart stuck in my throat.

I couldn't tell Rob.

He was fighting his own war with melanoma.

He had to stay strong.

He had to believe in his healing.

So I carried the weight—alone. I was with my father's long-time friend Jeanne at the time; I wouldn't know what I would do without her. We both looked at each other after the news, and we were in a state of shock.

I went to check on Dad.

Tubes hooked into his body.

Blood moving in and out.

He was conscious... but fading in and out.

I held his hand.

Tried not to shake.

And at the same time, just across the city,

Rob was in another hospital—still standing, still pushing, still believing he had a chance.

I didn't have the words.

I didn't have the faith.

I just had the responsibility.

The surgeon" had to remove several organs.

Said it was B-cell lymphoma—very aggressive.

Meanwhile, Rob had just finished chemo.

He was pale. Thin.

But his head was still high. His spirit still fighting.

Dad finally got out of the hospital a few weeks later.

We walked out of Dad's doctor's appointment together — him moving slowly, fragile but proud.

And then the phone rang again.

"Is this Shawn Patrick?"

"Yes..."

"We're calling from hospice. Your brother... he's not going to make it. The cancer has hit his spinal fluid. He'll be moved to in-care hospice."

I dropped the phone. Right there, in the doctor's office parking lot.

I sat on a bench and cried —

Shoulders shaking, fists clenched.

Dad sat next to me.

Still healing. Still praying.

But not to Rob.

To God.

I couldn't pray.

Not anymore.

Not when the last two men in my life were dying.

Not when I had no answers.

I had nothing left but questions.

"Why am I still here?"

"Why them and not me?"

"Why does God put this pain in my lap?"

I couldn't make sense of it.

I couldn't find peace in the Bible.

I couldn't even say thank you anymore.

I had lost my faith.

But even in that emptiness —

In the silence, the needles, the hospital chairs, the unanswered prayers, One word stayed with me: "WhyKnotUS"

It was the only thing keeping my hands busy,

Still working on the final kinks every single day of what it should look like.

The only thing that reminded me I still had a purpose.

And in that moment, it became more than a brand.

It became the only light I had left.

CHAPTER 12

The Walkkkk

A few months had passed.
Dad was still struggling. The surgery took so much out
of him—physically, mentally, spiritually. He spent most of his
days in bed, fighting quietly.

And me?

I was bartending in Manhattan, going through the motions.
Smiling on the outside. Empty inside.

I wasn't living. Just surviving.

To be honest, I felt lost. Confused. I had been to more
funerals than birthdays.

I couldn't sleep.

My mind wouldn't shut off.

So I started smoking a little weed before bed—just to take
the edge off.

But it started becoming more than just that.

I wasn't feeling like the strong version of me anymore.

I was slipping.

One Day, after a long shift at work, I felt like I had nothing left to give.

I walked out of the bar, headphones in. WhyKnotUS stickers on both sides of the headphones, like anchors holding me together.

And I just... walked.

Head down.

Music up.

One foot in front of the other.

I walked 51 blocks.

Didn't even realize it.

And then, on that 51st block... I looked up.

St. Patrick's Cathedral.

Massive. Quiet. Lit like a scene in a movie.

And something told me, "Go in."

I hadn't prayed in a long time.

Didn't know how anymore.

Too much had happened.

Too much had been lost.

But I walked in.

Not through the main aisle.

I kept going, deeper into the back.

Toward one of those small, private rooms for prayer.

I reached for the door.

I was wearing my glasses.

And just as I touched the handle, a bright light flashed off the right side of my lens.

So strong it stopped me.

I stepped back, took off my glasses, rubbed my eye.

And when I looked to my right...

I saw him.

A priest.

Standing alone.

His name was Father Donald Haggerty.

This is St. Patrick's Cathedral—one of the most sacred and hidden places in the world.

You never see a priest unless there's a service.

But there was no service.

He looked at me.

Locked eyes.

And I walked toward him.

He asked, "What can I help you with?"

I told him everything.

Everything.

The losses.

The guilt.

The brand.

The weed.

The pain.

The doubt.

He said, "Come downstairs with me."

We went into the chambers.

Quiet. Cold. Ancient.

It felt like I had stepped into another world.

He looked me in the eye and said "You haven't lost your faith. You've just been walking in the dark."

He told me to get rosary beads.
To come back to church every single day.
To pray.
To start clean.
To stop running.
That day... God saved my life.
And I've been at St. Patrick's every day since.
Not for people.
Not for validation.
Not for peace and quiet.
For God.
Because now?
I don't fear anyone.
I don't fear any situation.
The only thing I fear... is God.
And the only thing I carry now... is faith.
This story is no longer about pain.
Now?
It's about power.
It's about purpose.
It's about WhyKnotUS.

@SURVIOR

56

📍 CHINOOK WINDS CASINO RESORT

CHAPTER 13

60 Seconds

After the walk... after getting my faith back inside the echoing walls of St. Patrick's... I came home changed.

That's when I finally finished the WhyKnotUS logo.

The colors in the knot weren't just a design choice—they meant something.

They meant New York.

The background? A photo of the skyline out the window... the same window I looked through with Rob.

But even with the logo complete, I was stuck.

I had no idea how to get this message out.

How to reach people.

How to make this thing real.

And at the same time, life kept closing in.

After Rob died, something inside me cracked wide open.

I was living in a basement apartment, taking care of my father—still sick from Stage 4 B-cell lymphoma.

I bartended full-time. I cared for him full-time.

Bills piled up. Grief hung in the air like smoke.

I had lost almost everyone I loved:

My mother. My brother. My aunts. My grandmother.

And yet somehow... I was still standing.

Barely.

I had faith again, but I didn't have a roadmap.

I had a logo, but no platform.

I needed money—but more than that, I needed meaning.

Then I saw it.

An open casting call for the TV show Survivor. Portland, Oregon. Two thousand miles away.

No guarantees. No promises. Just one shot.

I packed light.

Tucked my rosary beads into the side pocket of my bag.

Booked a flight.

I flew across the country with nothing but a whisper of hope and a prayer in my back pocket.

When I landed, I still had a four-hour bus ride ahead of me.

Didn't matter. I rode that bus like it was taking me to destiny.

Outside the audition building, I stood in line for hours.

People laughed. Nervous energy everywhere.

Me?

I wasn't there to play Survivor.

I was there because I already was one.

They gave us 60 seconds in front of the camera. That's it.

And here's what I said:

Hello, my name is Shawn Patrick, and I am a bartender in NYC.

I flew across the country and took a four-hour bus ride just to stand in this line and talk to this camera for 60 seconds.

I did not just come here to play Survivor.

I am one.

I buried my mother when I was 13. I buried my brother a few months ago. I've lost just about every single person on this planet that I loved.

Right now, I'm taking care of my father who is fighting Stage 4 B-cell lymphoma.

I've been to more funerals than birthday parties.

I am mentally and physically ready for this moment.

So I'm asking you—put me on that island, and I will:

OUTWIT.

OUTPLAY.

OUTLAST whoever the hell is in front of me.

And I'll show the world that if you just believe in yourself,

Anything is possible.

That speech? It wasn't rehearsed.

It came straight from the gut.

I wasn't just trying to get cast. I was trying to fight for my life.

When I left Portland that night, I had no idea what was coming next.

No callback yet. No green light. No confirmation.

But I knew something had shifted.

Because for the first time...

I had stepped out of the shadows.

CHAPTER 14

Adoro Restaurant

W hen I came back from Portland, something shifted. The air out there was clean. My mind was clearer.

I didn't land a deal or get a call back—yet.

But I came home with a quiet kind of confidence, like I had touched something real.

And when I walked back into Adoro, my employer for the past year, I realized...

This wasn't just a restaurant. It was family.

Before I even left for Survivor auditions, the people at work were cheering me on.

Two of the owners—Rick and his son Antonio—kept asking me every day, "When do you leave?" "You ready for this?"

They were genuinely excited for me.

I showed them the 60-second speech I planned to deliver.

And when I looked up after reading it—

Tears filled their eyes.

They didn't even know the whole story.

Not about Rob. Not about Mom. Not about the pain I carried.

But they felt it.

Antonio looked at me, eyes glassy, and said, "I want to give you something."

He pulled out a set of brown rosary beads from his pocket.

Worn from time.

Held every day.

And passed down from the tomb of St. Francis.

I tried not to take them.

He insisted.

That moment right there?

That's when I knew:

I was meant to be in this restaurant.

This place.

This chapter of my life.

Because even when people didn't know what I was going through, they still saw my light.

And that meant the story—my story—needed to be told.

Then there's Mario.

The boss.

A 5-star Michelin chef. In the restaurant world, that's untouchable.

I'll never forget our interview.

He walked in wearing a Mets jersey.

Right then, I knew: We're going to connect.

Only two months into the job, Rob passed away.

And Mario showed up at the funeral.

I kept talking to him about WhyKnotUS.

About the logo.

About pitching it to the Mets—his team.

He loved it, but gave it to me straight. "It's a great idea. It really is. The Mets are underdogs. But with slogans and branding—teams move on. They always find the next thing."

That stuck with me.

Because this knot?

It wasn't a seasonal thing.

It wasn't just for the Mets.

It held the names of everyone I've lost.

It carried the weight of years.

It was my pain... my hope... my prayer.

I told him again, "My life is a movie."

He looked at me and said, "I know it is."

CHAPTER 15

First Row

Days after, I walked into St. Patrick's Cathedral like I always do.

But something was off.

I reached into my bag for my rosary beads—the same ones I always wrap around my hand when I pray. They weren't there.

I thought maybe they slipped into a pocket or got caught in my sweats, but deep down I knew—I forgot them.

And for a moment, it felt like I couldn't pray without them.

That grip, that connection, that anchor—it wasn't there.

I made my way to the small side room in the back, the one I always go to. But this time, something pulled me toward the first row.

I don't ever sit in the front. Never have.

It always felt like I didn't belong there—like the kid who avoids the first row in class because he doesn't want to get picked by the teacher. Maybe I didn't want to be seen. Or maybe I just didn't think I deserved to be up front.

But today, I walked right in, got on my knees, made the sign of the cross, and sat in that front row. I moved over to the side so there was room for someone else.

Then they came.

A mother and her three daughters.

They slid into the row beside me, and within minutes... the mother began to cry. Silent tears falling in front of her girls. The oldest, maybe ten years old, just folded her hands and kept praying. The two younger ones didn't fully understand, but they knew something was wrong.

And just like that — my heart cracked open.

I didn't know their story. I didn't know their pain.

But I felt it like it was my own.

And I prayed.

Not for me.

Not for strength or clarity or answers.

But for them.

And in that moment, everything about WhyKnotUS came into focus. But this revelation started the night of my conversation with Mario, the 5-star Michelin chef.

That night, the pieces of the puzzle started to fit together.

WhyKnotUS isn't just a pitch.

It isn't just a logo.

It's not just a brand.

It's not just a dream.

It's not about attention or deals or fame.

It's my story.

It's for...

The fighters.

The silent warriors.

The ones who keep pushing.

It's about hope.

It's about unity.

It's for the underdogs.

It's about belonging.

It's about the kid who sits in the back because life has picked on him too much.

It's about the mother who holds it together until she can't anymore.

It's about strangers sitting side by side, not knowing each other's story, but praying through the same storm.

WhyKnotUS is that front row.

It's that moment when you show up without your beads but realize you are the prayer now.

You don't need something in your hand when it already lives in your heart.

I didn't lose my rosary beads that day.

I was just being reminded...

That the real power isn't in what we hold.

It's in who we are when we show up anyway.

So I decided...

To stop whispering.

And start writing.

Because this story wasn't just mine anymore.

It was meant to be heard.

And maybe... just maybe—

All of this was leading me here.

To write this book.

So that someone out there holding on by a thread would finally hear this:

You're not alone.

And you're not done yet.

Refuse to fold.

CHAPTER 16

Why Knot You

You've read my story.
But this book was never just about me.
It's about you.
Maybe your pain doesn't look like mine.
Maybe your losses are different.
Maybe your knot is tied a little tighter, a little messier.
But it's still yours.
And you're still here.
That means something.
Everyone has a knot.
Some people carry grief.
Some carry guilt.
Some carry fear.
But if you're still breathing, still standing—
Then your story isn't over yet.
This isn't about being perfect.
It's about not giving up.
It's about waking up when you feel like staying in bed.

It's about showing up when no one's clapping.

It's about fighting through silence, through doubt, through everything that says "you can't," and saying, Why Knot Me?

If you can see it in your mind, You can hold it in your hand.

That's not a quote.

That's the truth.

So whether your knot is frayed, tangled, or barely holding together—

Just know this:

It's still strong enough to hold you.

And maybe, just maybe...

You were meant to read this.

You were meant to remember:

You are the story.

You are the reason.

You are WhyKnotUS.

About the Author

Shawn Patrick is a New York-raised storyteller, survivor, and creator of the movement Why Knot Us—a brand born from pain, perseverance, and the unbreakable bonds of family. Raised between the heart of the city and the weight of real-life loss, Shawn never followed the traditional path. From couch to couch, from funeral to funeral, he carried a dream that never let go.

He hustled outside stadiums, stood tall through trauma, and found purpose not in perfection but in resilience.

This memoir is not just a story—it's his truth. A journey from pain to purpose, from silence to strength, from underdog to unstoppable.

Why Knot Us is his message to the world: Why not the broken? Why not the bold? Why knot us?

> "You have not because you ask not."
> — James 4:2 (KJV)

I've learned that faith is not just about waiting; it's about moving, asking, and believing. This book is proof that when you step forward and ask, doors open.